ANGRY BIRDS

SEASONS

JOKE BOOK

EGMONT

We bring stories to life

First published in Great Britain 2013 by Egmont UK Limited
The Yellow Building, 1 Nicholas Road, London W11 4AN

ISBN 978 1 4052 6917 9
56733/1
Printed in Great Britain

VALEN-SWINE'S DAY

WHAT DID THE STAMP SAY TO THE ENVELOPE ON VALENTINE'S DAY?

I'm stuck on you!

WHY DID THE PIG GIVE HIS GIRLFRIEND A BOX OF CHOCOLATES?

It was Valen-swine's Day!

WHAT DID THE BOY BIRD SAY TO THE GIRL BIRD ON VALENTINE'S DAY?

Let me call you tweet-heart!

WHY DID THE BANANA GO OUT WITH THE PRUNE?

Because it couldn't get a date.

WHAT DID THE OVERWEIGHT PIG SAY TO HIS GIRLFRIEND?

I love you a ton!

HOGS AND KISSES

WHAT DID THE BAT SAY TO HIS GIRLFRIEND?

You're fun to hang around with.

WHAT DID THE BOY OWL SAY TO THE GIRL OWL ON VALENTINE'S DAY?

Owl be yours!

KNOCK, KNOCK!

Who's there?

SHERWOOD.

Sherwood who?

SHERWOOD LIKE TO BE YOUR VALENTINE!

KNOCK, KNOCK!
Who's there?
OLIVE.
Olive who?
OLIVE YOU, TOO!

WHAT DID THE BOY SQUIRREL SAY TO THE GIRL SQUIRREL ON VALENTINE'S DAY?
I'm nuts about you!

WHAT DID THE GIRL SQUIRREL SAY BACK?
You're nuts so bad yourself!

WHY DOESN'T BOMB LIKE TALKING TO GIRLS?
He's worried there'd be a spark between them!

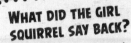

WHAT KIND OF DATE DOES CHUCK LIKE TO GO ON?
Speed dating!

HOGS AND KISSES 2

WHAT DID THE CHOCOLATE SYRUP SAY TO THE ICE CREAM?

I'm sweet on you!

WHAT HAPPENED TO THE COUPLE WHO MET IN A REVOLVING DOOR?

They're still going around together!

WHY DID MINION PIG BREAK UP WITH HIS GIRLFRIEND?

He was green with envy!

HOW DID THE TELEPHONE PROPOSE TO HIS GIRLFRIEND?

He gave her a ring.

WHAT DID ONE LIGHT BULB SAY TO THE OTHER?

I love you a whole watt!

WHY DID MINION PIG HAVE HIS GIRLFRIEND PUT IN JAIL?

She stole his heart.

WHAT DID ONE SNAKE SAY TO THE OTHER SNAKE?

Give me a hiss!

WHAT DID ONE FISH SAY TO THE OTHER FISH?

You're quite a catch!

WHAT DID RED SAY TO KING PIG?

Watch out, I'm about to get a crush on you!

KNOCK, KNOCK!

Who's there?

HOWARD.

Howard who?

HOWARD YOU LIKE A GREAT BIG KISS?

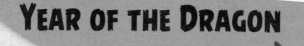

YEAR OF THE DRAGON

HOW DID THE DRAGON WIN THE TALENT CONTEST?
She was the beast in the show!

WHAT DO YOU DO WITH A GREEN DRAGON?
Wait until it ripens!

WHAT DO THE PIGS THINK OF MIGHTY DRAGON?
He makes them sizzle!

WHERE DID THE DRAGON LEARN TO BREATHE FIRE?
At knight school!

WHAT'S PURPLE, 10,000 KM LONG AND 12 M HIGH?
The grape wall of China.

WHAT DID THE DRAGON SAY WHEN HE SAW A KNIGHT IN SHINING ARMOUR?

Oh no, not more tinned food!

WHY DID THE DRAGON CROSS THE ROAD?

Because he'd scared away all the chickens!

THE BLUES WON'T GO TO SCHOOL!

They'll go, even if I end up dragon them there myself!

WHAT DO YOU DO WHEN A DRAGON SNEEZES?

Get out of the way!

WHAT DID THE DRAGON SAY TO THE PIECE OF BREAD?

You're toast!

YEAR OF THE DRAGON 2

WHAT'S BLACK AND WHITE AND GOES ROUND AND ROUND?
A panda stuck in a revolving door.

WHAT DO CHINESE DRAGONS EAT FOR BREAKFAST?
Panda-cakes!

KNOCK, KNOCK,
Who's there?
DRAGON.
Dragon who?
STOP DRAGON YOUR FEET AND OPEN THE DOOR!

WHY DO DRAGONS SLEEP DURING THE DAY?
So they can fight knights.

SILLY SPRING!

WHEN DO MONKEYS FALL FROM THE SKY?

During Ape-ril showers!

WHY DID RED GO TO THE HOSPITAL?

He needed tweetment!

WHY IS EVERYONE SO TIRED ON APRIL 1ST?

Because they've just finished a 31 day March!

WHICH FLOWER GROWS UNDER YOUR NOSE?

Tulips!

WHY DID THE CHICK DISAPPOINT HIS MOTHER?

He wasn't what he was cracked up to be.

WHAT DO YOU CALL A LAMB WITH NO LEGS?

A cloud.

WHAT DID THE OWL SAY IN THE SPRING SHOWER?

"Too-wet-to-woo!"

CAN FEBRUARY MARCH?

No, but April May!

HOW MANY LAMBS DOES IT TAKE TO KNIT A SWEATER?

Don't be silly – lambs can't knit!

WHY IS THE LETTER A LIKE A FLOWER?

Because a B comes after it!

WHAT DO YOU GET IF YOU CROSS A BOA CONSTRICTOR AND A SHEEP?

A wrap-around jumper!

DO YOU KNOW ALL ABOUT APRIL 1ST?

Yes, I'm fool-y aware of it!

HOPPITY SLOP!

WHAT DO YOU CALL A GIRL WITH A FROG ON HER HEAD?

Lily!

HOW DO YOU KNOW CARROTS ARE GOOD FOR YOUR EYES?

Because you never see a rabbit wearing glasses!

WHY DID THE BUNNY BUILD HERSELF A NEW HOUSE?

She was fed up with the hole thing.

WHAT DID THE RABBIT GIVE HIS GIRLFRIEND?

A 14 carrot ring!

DID YOU HEAR ABOUT THE RICH RABBIT?

He was a million-hare!

WHAT IS A RABBIT'S FAVORITE DANCE STYLE?

Hip hop!

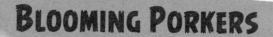

BLOOMING PORKERS

HOW DO TREES GET ON THE INTERNET?

They log on!

WHY IS KING PIG LIKE A FLOWER?

He rose to power!

I JUST BOUGHT A NEW BOOK ON GARDENING.

Why?

BECAUSE I WANT TO BE A GOOD WEEDER!

EGGS-CITING EASTER

WHY IS THE EASTER BUNNY SO CLEVER?

He's an egghead!

WHY COULDN'T THE EASTER EGG FAMILY WATCH TV?

Because their signal was scrambled.

HOW LONG DO THE ANGRY BIRDS WORK ON EASTER SUNDAY?

Around the cluck!

WHAT DO YOU CALL A SLEEPY ANGRY BIRD?

Egg-sausted!

HOW SHOULD YOU SEND A LETTER TO THE EASTER BUNNY?

By hare mail!

WHERE DOES THE EASTER BUNNY GET HIS EGGS?

From Eggplants!

EGGS-CITING EASTER 2

WHAT'S LONG, STYLISH AND FULL OF CATS?
The Easter Purr-rade!

DID YOU HEAR ABOUT THE FARMER WHO FED CRAYONS TO HIS CHICKENS?
He wanted them to lay colourful eggs for Easter!

WHY DO PEOPLE PAINT EASTER EGGS?
Because it's easier than wallpapering them!

THERE WAS A ROOSTER SITTING ON A TOP OF A BARN. IF IT LAID AN EGG, WHICH WAY WOULD IT ROLL?
Roosters don't lay eggs!

HOW DO THE ANGRY BIRDS FIND THEIR PRECIOUS EGGS?
Eggs mark the spot!

St. Patrick's Day Honkers

Why do people wear shamrocks on St. Patrick's Day?

Because real rocks are too heavy.

Why shouldn't you iron a four-leaf clover?

Because you don't want to press your luck.

Knock, knock!

Who's there?

Irish.

Irish Who?

Irish you a happy St. Patrick's Day!

Are people jealous of the Irish?

Sure, they're green with envy!

What would you get if you crossed Christmas with St. Patrick's Day?

St. O'Claus!

WHY ARE LEPRECHAUNS SO HARD TO GET ALONG WITH?
Because they're very short-tempered!

IS IT LUCKY WHEN YOU FIND A HORSESHOE?

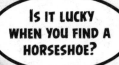

Not for the horse!

HOW IS A BEST FRIEND LIKE A FOUR-LEAF CLOVER?
Because they are hard to find and lucky to have.

WHY IS A RIVER ALWAYS LUCKY WITH MONEY?
It has two banks!

WHY DO LEPRECHAUNS MAKE GOOD JOURNALISTS?
They're great at shorthand!

FOUR CHEEP CLOVER

WHY CAN'T YOU BORROW MONEY FROM A LEPRECHAUN?
Because they are always a little short.

WHO'S THE LUCKIEST ANGRY BIRD?
The one at the end of the queue!

WHY DO PIGS HIDE BEHIND FOUR-LEAF CLOVERS?
They need all the luck they can get!

SIZZLING SUMMER SIDE-SPLITTERS!

WHERE DO RETIRED PIGS GO IN THE SUMMER?
To the tro-pigs!

WHERE DOES A SHIP GO WHEN IT'S SICK?
To the dock!

WHAT DO YOU CALL A BIRD WHO IS OUT OF BREATH IN THE HOT SUN?
A puffin!

WHAT'S THE BEST DAY TO GO TO THE BEACH?
Sun-day!

WHY DO FISH SWIM IN SALT WATER?
Because pepper makes them sneeze!

WHY ARE GULLS NAMED SEAGULLS?
If they were in the bay, they'd be bagels!

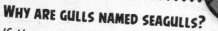

WHY DID THE TEACHER WEAR SUNGLASSES?

Because his class was so bright!

WHAT DOES A POTATO DO WHEN IT'S HOT?

Take off its jacket!

WHY DO BANANAS USE SUNCREAM?

Because they peel!

WHAT DO WHALES EAT WITH ICE CREAM?

Jellyfish!

WHY DID THE PIG GO ON HOLIDAY ON HIS OWN?

Because all his friends at home were taking him for grunted!

WHERE DOES A FISH GO TO BORROW MONEY?

A loan shark!

HOLIDAY TWEETS!

HOW DID THE BIRD CRASH-LAND ON THE DESERT ISLAND?

With its sparrow-chute!

WHAT'S BLACK, WHITE AND RED ALL OVER?

A penguin with sunburn!

HOW DO SAILORS WASH THEIR CLOTHES?

They throw their laundry overboard and it's washed ashore!

WHAT'S A GOOD HOLIDAY TIP?
Never catch snowflakes in your mouth until the birds have flown south for the winter!

WHAT FLIES THROUGH THE JUNGLE SINGING OPERA?
The parrots of Penzance.

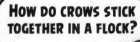

HOW DO CROWS STICK TOGETHER IN A FLOCK?
Vel-crow!

SUMMER PIG-NICS

WHERE DO PIGS EAT THEIR PICNICS IN NEW YORK?

Central Pork!

WHAT DO YOU CALL A DOG ON THE BEACH IN SUMMER?

A hot dog!

WHAT DID THE PIG SAY ON A HOT DAY?

I'm bacon!

WHERE DO THE PIGS GO ON HOLIDAY?

The Cook Islands

WHAT'S THE BEST TYPE OF FOOD TO EAT TO KEEP COOL?

Chilli!

WHERE CAN YOU LEARN HOW TO MAKE ICE CREAM?

At sundae school.

WHERE DO DOGS GO ON HOLIDAY?

A theme bark!

WHAT DO THE ANGRY BIRDS GET IN A HEATWAVE?

Boiled eggs!

KNOCK, KNOCK!

Who's there?

ICE CREAM SODA.

Ice cream soda who?

ICE CREAM SODA PEOPLE CAN HEAR ME!

HOW DO YOU GET A FISH TO KEEP A SECRET?

Ask it not to tell a sole!

HAPPY BIRD-DAY

WHAT DID THE PIG SAY WHEN HE OPENED HIS BIRTHDAY PRESENT?

That snout my style.

WHAT'S A PARROT'S FAVOURITE BIRTHDAY GAME?

Hide and speak!

WHAT DOES EVERY BIRTHDAY END WITH?

y!

WHAT DO YOU ALWAYS GET ON YOUR BIRTHDAY?

Another year older!

WHAT DID THE ELEPHANT WISH FOR ON HIS BIRTHDAY?

A trunk full of gifts!

WHAT IS A PIG'S FAVOURITE TYPE OF PARTY?

A sow-prize party!

WHAT DID ONE CANDLE SAY TO THE OTHER?
Don't birthdays burn you up?

HAL: I get heartburn every time I eat birthday cake.

RED: Next time don't eat the candles!

WHAT GOES UP AND NEVER COMES DOWN?

Your age!

KNOCK, KNOCK.

Who's there?

ABBY.

Abby who?

ABBY BIRTHDAY!

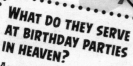

WHAT DO THEY SERVE AT BIRTHDAY PARTIES IN HEAVEN?

Angel cake, of course!

WHAT DO YOU GIVE A 900-POUND GORILLA FOR HIS BIRTHDAY?

I don't know, but you'd better hope he likes it!

HAPPY BIRD-DAY AGAIN!

WHY DO WE PUT CANDLES ON TOP OF A BIRTHDAY CAKE?

Because it's too hard to put them on the bottom!

WHAT DOES A CRAB DO ON HIS BIRTHDAY?

He shellabrates!

WHAT DID THE ICE-CREAM SAY TO THE UNHAPPY BIRTHDAY CAKE?

What's eating you?

WHAT DOES A CAT LIKE TO EAT ON HIS BIRTHDAY?

Jelly and mice cream!

WHAT KIND OF TIE DOES A PIG WEAR ON ITS BIRTHDAY?

A pig's-tie!

WHAT DID THE BALD MAN SAY WHEN HE GOT A COMB FOR HIS BIRTHDAY?

Thanks. I'll never part with it!

WHAT DID THE BIRTHDAY BALLOON SAY TO THE PIN?

Hello, Buster!

WHAT BIRD EATS THE MOST BIRTHDAY CAKE?

The swallow.

WHY ARE BIRTHDAYS GOOD FOR YOU?

Because people who have the most birthdays live the longest!

MATILDA: When's your birthday?

HAL: December 11th.

MATILDA: What year?

HAL: Every year!

AUTUMNAL ANTICS

WHAT DID THE BIRD SAY WHEN ALL THE LEAVES TURNED GOLD AND RED?

This is very pheasant!

WHAT DID ONE LEAF SAY TO ANOTHER?

I'm falling for you.

WHY DID THE PIG CUT A HOLE IN HIS UMBRELLA?

He wanted to be able to tell when it had stopped raining!

THE BIRDS DON'T LIKE WEARING RAINCOATS... THEY'VE GOT ANORAK-NAPHOBIA!

WHAT ALWAYS FALLS DOWN IN AUTUMN?

Leaves!

WHAT DID THE BIRD SAY WHEN SHE SAW A BIG OAK TREE?

"That's probably the best tree I have feather seen."

WHAT DID THE BEAVER SAY TO THE TREE?

It's been nice gnawing you!

WHAT DID THE TREE WEAR TO THE POOL PARTY?

Swimming trunks!

WHAT IS A TREE'S LEAST FAVOURITE MONTH?

Sep-timber!

WHY DID THE LEAF GO TO THE DOCTOR?

It was feeling green!

WHAT KIND OF TREE CAN FIT INTO YOUR HAND?

A palm tree!

WHAT IS GREEN AND PECKS ON TREES?

Woody Wood-pickle!

MORE AUTUMNAL ANTICS

WHAT DID THE BIRD SAY TO HER FRIEND WHEN SHE NEEDED HELP COLLECTING BERRIES?

Can you sparrow a minute?

HOW CAN YOU TELL THAT A TREE IS A DOGWOOD TREE?

By its bark!

WHAT KIND OF PANTS DO CLOUDS PUT ON?

Thunder-wear!

WHAT FALLS BUT NEVER HITS THE GROUND?

The temperature!

WHAT DID THE CLOUD SAY TO THE LIGHTNING BOLT?

You're shocking!

WHEN DOES IT RAIN MONEY?

When there's a change in the weather.

WHO DOES EVERYONE LISTEN TO, BUT NO ONE BELIEVES?

The weatherman.

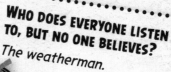

DID YOU HEAR THE ONE ABOUT THE OAK TREE?

It's a-corny one!

WHAT DO YOU CALL IT WHEN IT RAINS CHICKENS AND DUCKS?

Foul weather!

WHAT DID THE BIRD SAY WHEN HE WAS ASKED TO MIGRATE TO AUSTRALIA?

That's ostrich too far.

BACK TO SCHOOL!

WHO'S THE LEADER OF SCHOOL STATIONERY?

The ruler!

WHAT KIND OF SCHOOL DOES A SURFER GO TO?

Boarding school!

WHAT KIND OF SCHOOL DOES A GIANT GO TO?

High school!

HOW CAN YOU MAKE SO MANY MISTAKES IN JUST ONE DAY?

I get up early!

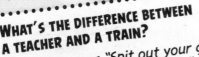

WHAT'S THE DIFFERENCE BETWEEN A TEACHER AND A TRAIN?

A teachers says "Spit out your gum!" and a train says "Chew! Chew!"

WHAT WOULD HAPPEN IF YOU TOOK THE SCHOOL BUS HOME?

The headmaster would make you bring it back!

WHY DID THE STUDENT THROW HIS WATCH OUT OF THE WINDOW?

He wanted to see time fly.

WHY IS A MATHS BOOK ALWAYS UNHAPPY?

Because it has a lot of problems!

WHAT DID THE PIGS DO AFTER SCHOOL?

Ham-work!

WHY DID THE STUDENT TAKE A LADDER TO SCHOOL?

He wanted to get a higher education!

HAM'O'WEEN

HOW DO YOU FIX A BROKEN PUMPKIN?

With a pumpkin patch!

WHAT IS A VAMPIRE'S SWEETHEART CALLED?

His ghoul-friend!

WHAT DO YOU GET IF YOU CROSS A SNOWMAN WITH A VAMPIRE?

Frostbite!

WHAT DID THE MUMMY SAY TO THE DETECTIVE?

Let's wrap this case up!

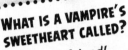

WHY DID THE VAMPIRES HAVE TO CANCEL THEIR GAME OF CRICKET?

Because they couldn't find their bats!

WHAT'S THE SPOOKIEST MATHS PROBLEM?

Pumpkin Pi!

HOW DO MONSTERS TELL THEIR FUTURE?

They read their horror-scope!

WHAT DID THE PIGS SERVE AT THEIR HALLOWEEN PARTY?

I scream!

WHY DON'T MUMMIES HAVE HOBBIES?

Because they're too wrapped up in their work!

WHY DID THE CYCLOPS GIVE UP TEACHING?

Because he only had one pupil!

ANGRY BIRD: What are you dressed up as?

OWL: You figure it hoot.

FRIGHT NIGHT!

WHAT SHOULD YOU DO WHEN ZOMBIES SURROUND YOUR HOUSE?

Hope it's Halloween!

WHAT DO YOU CALL A WITCH AT THE BEACH?

A sand-witch.

WHAT DO THE ANGRY BIRDS LIKE TO DO ON HALLOWEEN?

Go trick or tweeting!

WHAT HAPPENED WHEN THE YOUNG WITCH MISBEHAVED?

She was sent to her broom.

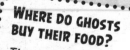

WHERE DO GHOSTS BUY THEIR FOOD?

The ghost-ery store!

WHAT DO WITCHES PUT ON THEIR HAIR?

Scare-spray!

WHY DO PIGS LOVE HALLOWEEN?

There's lots of hogs gobblin'!

WHY IS A WITCH LIKE AN ANGRY BIRD?

They both like to fly off the handle!

WHERE DO PIGS LIKE TO GO TRICK OR TREATING?

In their neigh-boar hood!

WHERE DO ZOMBIES LIKE TO GO SWIMMING?

The Dead Sea!

WHAT MAKES A SKELETON LAUGH?

When someone tickles its funny bone!

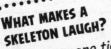

FRIGHT NIGHT PART 2

WHY DID THE MUMMY FEEL TENSE?

He was all wound up!

WHEN DOES A GHOST LIKE TO HAVE BREAKFAST?

In the moaning.

WHAT KIND OF ROADS DO GHOSTS HAUNT?

Dead ends.

WHAT DO BABY GHOSTS WEAR ON THEIR FEET?

Boo-ties!

WHY CAN'T SKELETONS HELP THE ANGRY BIRDS DEFEAT THE PIGS?

They have no guts!

WHAT DID THE PIG WEAR TO DRESS UP AS A VAMPIRE?

Ma-scare-a!

WHERE DO BABY GHOSTS GO?

Day-scare!

WHY DID THE HEADLESS HORSEMAN GO INTO BUSINESS?

He wanted to get ahead in life!

WHAT DO GHOSTS EAT FOR BREAKFAST?

Spook-ghetti!

WHERE DO GHOSTS LIKE TO PARTY?

Anywhere they can boo-gie!

WHAT IS DRACULA'S LEAST-FAVOURITE SONG?

You are my sunshine!

WHAT INSTRUMENT DO SKELETONS PLAY?

The trombone!

WHAT'S IT LIKE TO BE BITTEN BY A VAMPIRE?

A bit of a pain in the neck!

WHY DOES DRACULA TAKE COLD MEDICINE?

He can't stop coffin!

WHAT IS A WITCH'S BEST SUBJECT AT SCHOOL?

Spelling!

HAPPY BIRD-DAY ONCE MORE!

RED: I guess I didn't get my birthday wish.

KING PIG: How do you know?

RED: You're still here!

WHERE DO YOU FIND A BIRTHDAY PRESENT FOR A CAT?

In a cat-alogue!

HOW CAN YOU TELL IF AN ELEPHANT HAS BEEN TO YOUR BIRTHDAY PARTY?

Look for his footprints in the ice cream.

WHERE DOES A SNOWMAN PUT HIS BIRTHDAY CANDLES?

On his birthday flake!

WHAT DID THE BIG CANDLE SAY TO THE LITTLE CANDLE?

You're too young to go out!

WINTER TICKLERS

WHY DO THE PIGS LOVE ICY WEATHER?

It makes it easier for them to slip away!

WHAT DID THE BIG FURRY HAT SAY TO THE WARM WOOLLY SCARF?

You hang around while I go on ahead.

WHY DO BIRDS FLY SOUTH IN WINTER?

Because it's too far to walk!

WHAT DO YOU CALL A REINDEER WITH NO EYES?

I have no eye deer.

WHAT VEGETABLE WAS FORBIDDEN ON THE SHIPS OF ARCTIC EXPLORERS?

Leeks!

WHY DOES IT TAKE LONGER TO BUILD A SNOWPIG THAN A SNOWBIRD?

You have to hollow the head out, first!

SHIVERY SIDE-SPLITTERS!

WHAT DO WOMEN USE TO STAY YOUNG LOOKING IN THE ARCTIC?

Cold cream!

WHAT SITS ON THE BOTTOM OF THE ARCTIC OCEAN AND SHAKES?

A nervous wreck.

WHAT DO PENGUINS EAT FOR LUNCH?

Ice-burgers!

HOW DO YOU AVOID GETTING COLD FEET?

Don't go around brrr-footed!

WHY AREN'T PENGUINS AS LUCKY AS THE ANGRY BIRDS?

The poor old penguins can't go south for the winter!

HOW DO YOU KNOW IF THERE'S A SNOWMAN IN YOUR BED?
You wake up with a cold!

WHAT DO YOU CALL FIFTY PENGUINS IN THE ARCTIC?
Lost! (They live in the Antarctic!)

WHY ARE LAPTOPS USELESS IN THE WINTER?
Their screens get frozen!

KNOCK, KNOCK!
Who's there?
FREEZE.
Freeze who?
FREEZE A JOLLY GOOD FELLOW!

WHAT DID THE POLICE OFFICER SAY WHEN HE SAW JACK FROST STEALING?
Freeze!

SNOWY TWEETS

WHAT'S BLACK, WHITE, BLACK, WHITE, BLACK, WHITE, BLACK, WHITE?

A penguin rolling down a hill!

WHY DO PENGUINS CARRY FISH IN THEIR BEAKS?

Because they haven't got any pockets.

KNOCK, KNOCK!

Who's there?

KEN.

Ken who?

KEN I STAY HOME FROM SCHOOL TODAY? IT'S TOO COLD TO GO OUTSIDE!

SEASON'S GREED-INGS

HOW DID THE PIGS SCARE THE SNOWMAN?

They showed it a hairdryer!

WHAT DO YOU CALL SANTA WHEN HE STOPS MOVING?

Santa Pause!

HOW MUCH DID SANTA PAY FOR HIS SLEIGH?

Nothing, it was on the house!

WHY DO MUMMIES LIKE CHRISTMAS SO MUCH?

Because of all the wrapping!

WHY ARE CHRISTMAS TREES SUCH BAD KNITTERS?

They are always dropping their needles.

WHAT DID THE GHOST SING TO FATHER CHRISTMAS?

I'll have a boo Christmas without you.

WHAT DO THEY SING UNDER THE OCEAN IN DECEMBER?

Christmas corals!

WHAT DO YOU GET IF YOU CROSS MISTLETOE AND A DUCK?

A Christmas quacker!

WHERE DOES A SNOWMAN KEEP HIS MONEY?

In a snow bank!

WRECK THE HALLS!

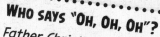

WHO SAYS "OH, OH, OH"?
Father Christmas walking backwards!

WHY DOES SANTA HAVE THREE GARDENS?
So he can hoe, hoe, hoe.

WHAT DO SNOWMEN EAT FOR BREAKFAST?
Frosted Flakes!

KING PIG: What's the best key to get at Christmas?

MINION: I don't know, great leader.

KING PIG: A turkey!

WHAT'S THE BEST THING TO GIVE YOUR PARENTS FOR CHRISTMAS?
A list of everything you want!

HO, HO, HO!

WHAT KIND OF BIRD CAN WRITE?
A pen-guin

WHY DID THE ELF PUSH HIS BED INTO THE FIREPLACE?
Because he wanted to sleep like a log!

WHAT DID THE CHRISTMAS TREE SAY TO THE PLUG?
You light me up!

WHAT DO YOU GET WHEN YOU EAT CHRISTMAS DECORATIONS?
Tinsilitis!

WHAT DID THE CHRISTMAS TREE SAY TO THE DECORATION?
Aren't you tired of hanging around?

WHAT'S WHITE, RED AND BLUE AT CHRISTMAS TIME?
A sad candy cane!

KNOCK, KNOCK.
Who's there?
DONUT.
Donut who?
DONUT OPEN UNTIL CHRISTMAS!

WHAT DO ANGRY MICE SEND TO EACH OTHER IN DECEMBER?
Cross mouse cards!

SEASONAL TWEETINGS

WHAT DO YOU GET IF YOU CROSS SANTA WITH A DETECTIVE?

Santa Clues!

WHAT DID ADAM SAY ON THE DAY BEFORE CHRISTMAS?

It's Christmas, Eve.

WHAT IS THE FEAR OF SANTA CLAUS CALLED?

Claus-trophobia

KNOCK, KNOCK!

Who's there?

SNOW.

Snow who?

SNOW USE - I'VE FORGOTTEN MY NAME AGAIN!

WHAT HAPPENED WHEN THE SNOWWOMAN GOT ANGRY AT THE SNOWMAN?

She gave him the cold shoulder.

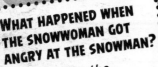

HOW DOES GOOD KING WENCESLAS LIKE HIS PIZZAS?

Deep pan, crisp and even!

WHAT DO SANTA'S ELVES DO AFTER SCHOOL?

Their gnomework!

WHY DOES FATHER CHRISTMAS LIKE TO GO DOWN THE CHIMNEY?

Because it soots him!

RED: What's the difference between the Christmas alphabet and the normal alphabet?

HAL: Dunno!

RED: The Christmas alphabet has no L!

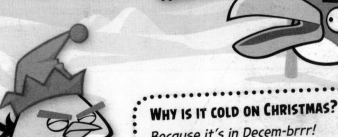

WHY IS IT COLD ON CHRISTMAS?

Because it's in Decem-brrr!

ANGRY BIRDS™

HOG ALL THE CHEEP LAUGHS WITH THE OFFICIAL ANGRY BIRDS SPACE JOKE BOOK

SCOUT FOR SNOUTS & SEEK SOME BEAKS IN ANGRY BIRDS SEARCH AND FIND!

VISIT WWW.EGMONT.CO.UK

OUT NOW